Ready·Set·Learn

Dot·to·Dot Alphabet

Grade K

180+ Stickers Inside

Managing Editor
Ina Massler Levin, M.A.

Editor
Eric Migliaccio

Contributing Editor
Sarah Smith

Creative Director
Karen J. Goldfluss, M.S. Ed.

Cover Design
Tony Carrillo / Marilyn Goldberg

Teacher Created Resources, Inc.
6421 Industry Way
Westminster, CA 92683
www.teachercreated.com

ISBN: 978-1-4206-5956-6

©2007 Teacher Created Resources, Inc.
Reprinted, 2009

Made in U.S.A.

Teacher Created Resources

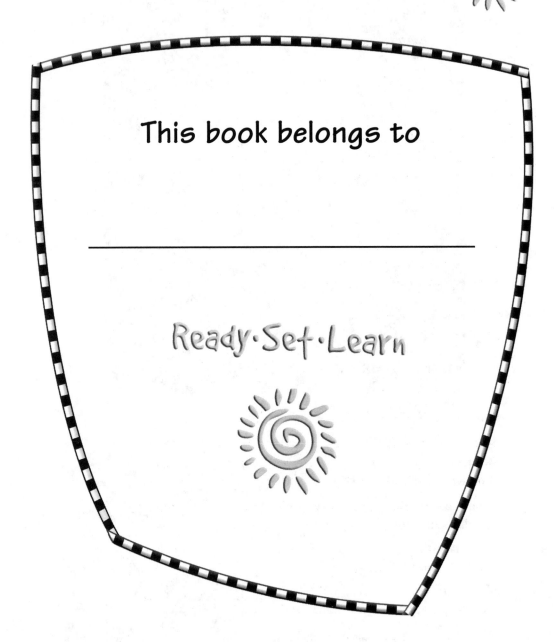

This book belongs to

_____

Ready·Set·Learn

Get Ready to Learn!

Get ready, get set, and go! Boost your child's learning with this exciting series of books. Geared to help children practice and master many needed skills, the *Ready·Set·Learn* books are bursting with 64 pages of learning fun. Use these books for . . .

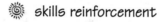

  ☀ enrichment   ☀ skills reinforcement   ☀ extra practice

With their smaller size, the *Ready·Set·Learn* books fit easily in children's hands, backpacks, and book bags. All your child needs to get started are pencils, crayons, and colored pencils.

A full sheet of colorful stickers is included. Use these stickers for . . .

  ☀ decorating pages

  ☀ rewarding outstanding effort

  ☀ keeping track of completed pages

Celebrate your child's progress by using these stickers on the reward chart located on the inside cover. The blue-ribbon sticker fits perfectly on the certificate on page 64.

With *Ready·Set·Learn* and a little encouragement, your child will be on the fast track to learning fun!

Circus Tricks (a–e)

Flower Pot (a–g)

Queen's Crown (a–i)

d
•

f
•

b
•

h
•

c
•

e
•

g
•

a ★

i

6

Under the Sea (a–j)

High Flyer (a–l)

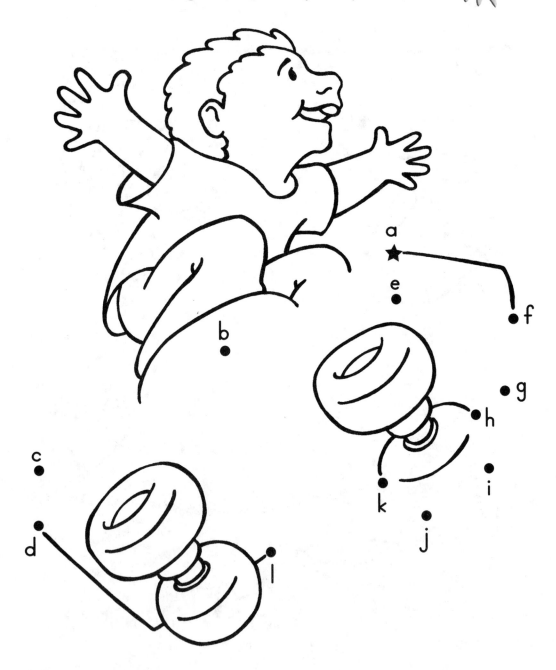

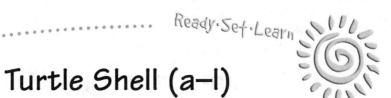

Turtle Shell (a–l)

Toothbrush (a–l)

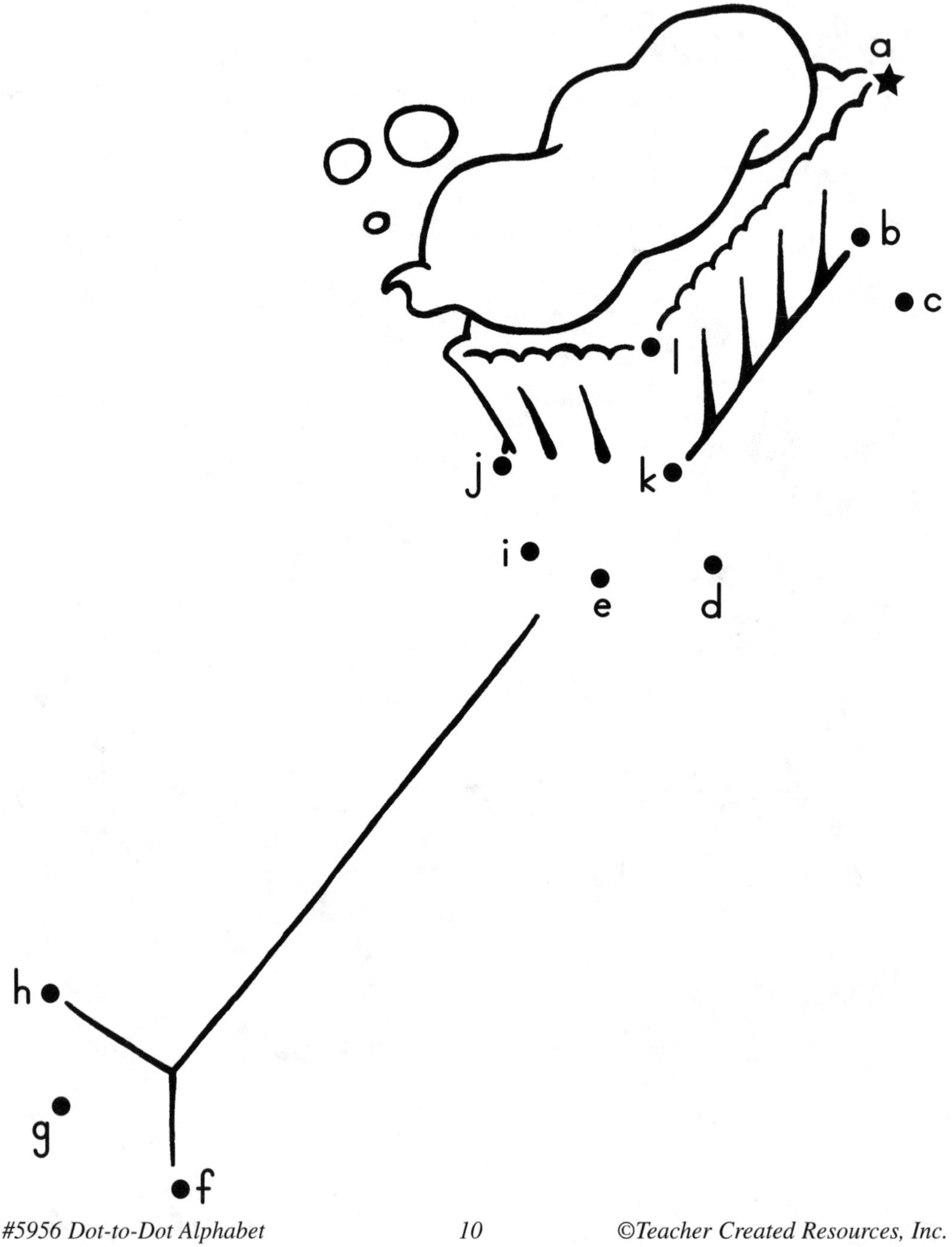

a

b

c

l

j

k

i

e

d

h

g

f

Mushroom (a–m)

g
•

• f

h •

i •

k   c

• e

j •   • d

b •

• l

m •

a ★

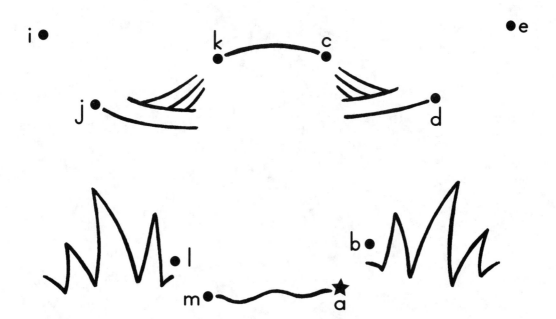

Butterfly (a–n)

b
•

•m

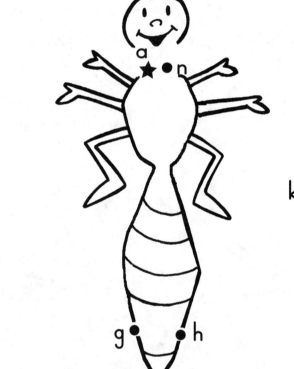

c
•

•l

d•

k•

•j

e
•

g• •h

•i

f
•

It's for Luck (a–o)

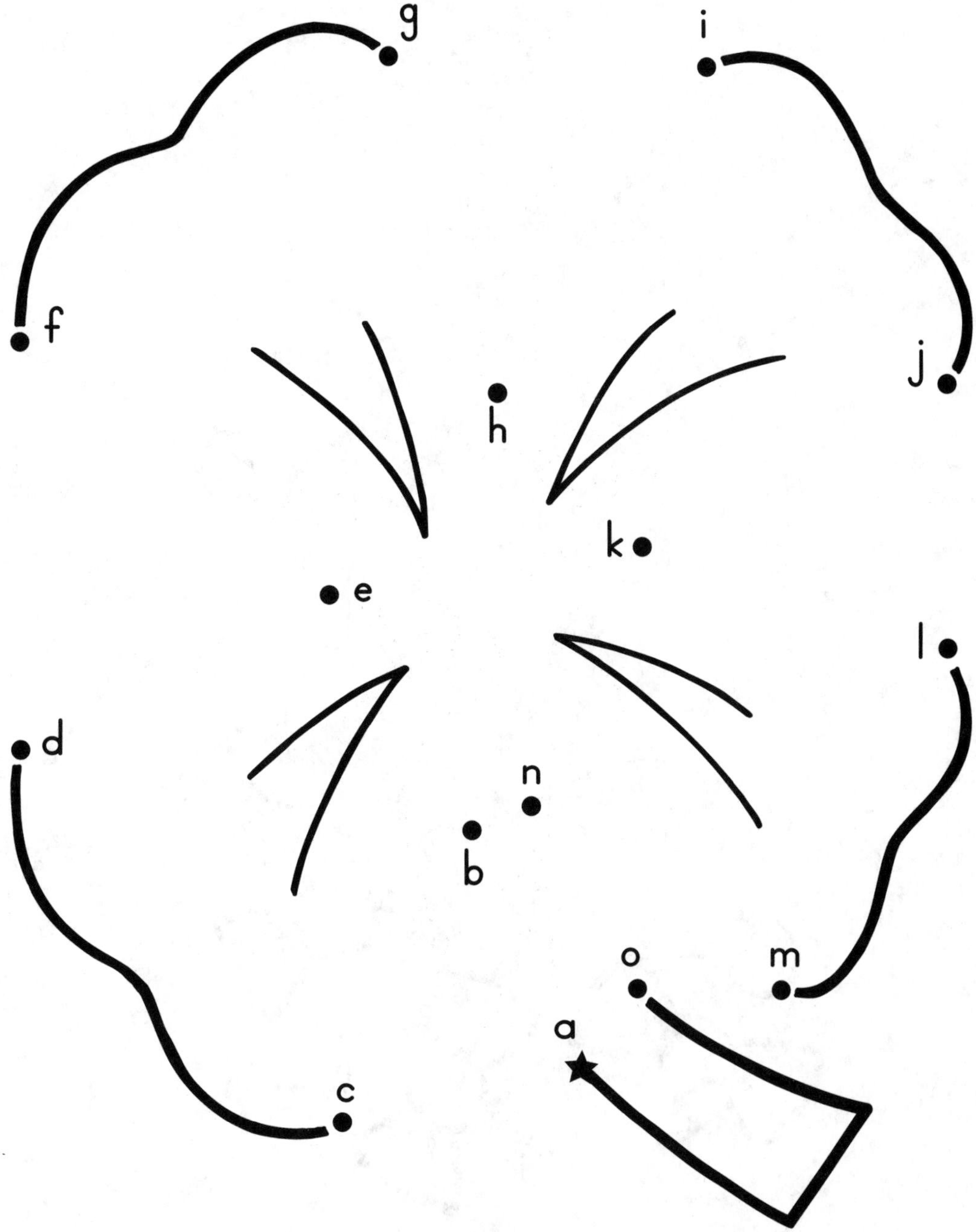

g

i

f

j

h

k

e

l

d

n

b

m

o

a

c

Flying High (a–p)

m

C •n

l•

o•

•f

g• •d

•e

a

•c

p• •k

•b

•h

j

i

Drink It Up (a–q)

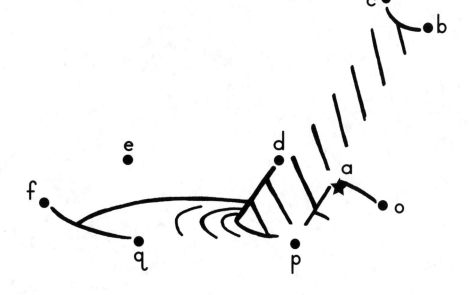

g●

●n

h●

●m

_____   _____

i●   ●l

j ●   ● k

Caterpillar (a-q)

Sliding Down (a–t)

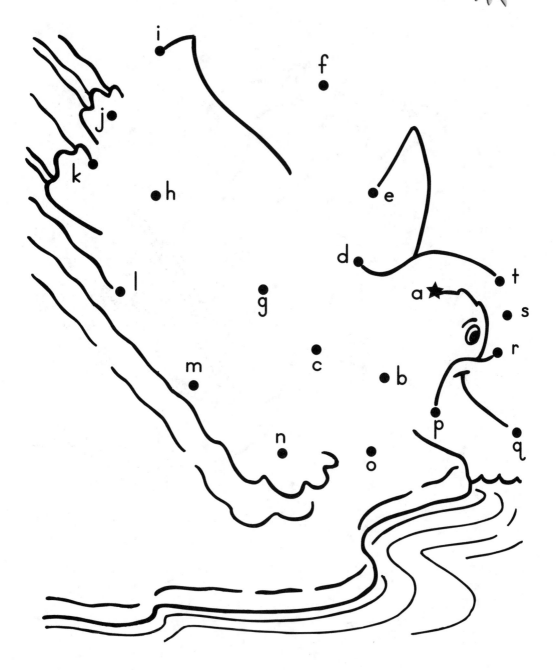

Downhill Skier (a–t)

Down the Tracks (a–t)

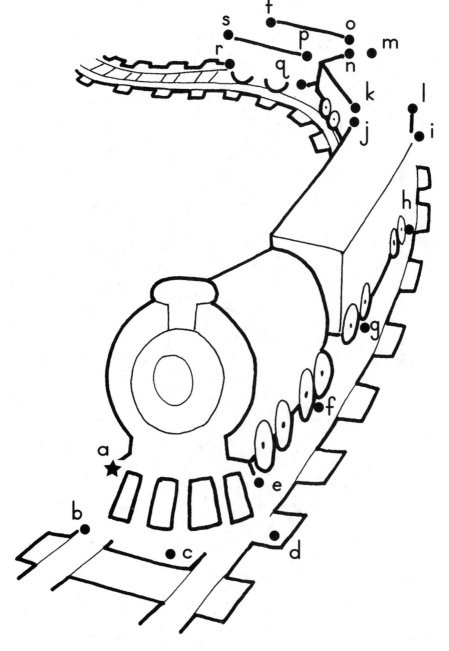

Mouse (a–t)

d

e

f

c

b

g

h

i

j

a

k

s

t

r

p

q

l

n

o

m

Bird in a Cage (a–t)

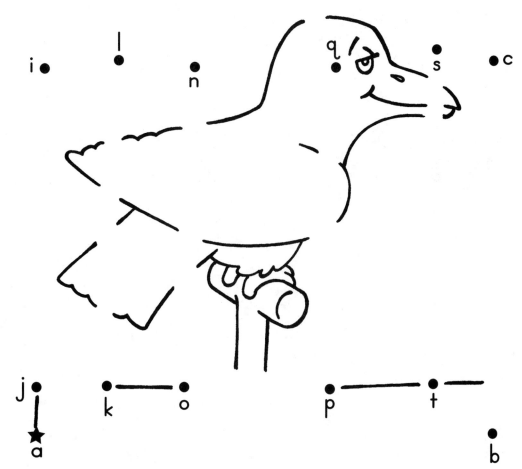

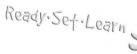

Pear (a–t)

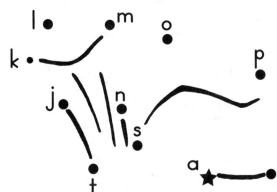

l • • m • o   • q

k •   p •

j •   • n
                s
i •   • t

                a ★——• r

                        b •

h •

                            • c

g •

f •

                        • d

        • e

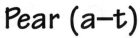

Lock and Key (a–v)

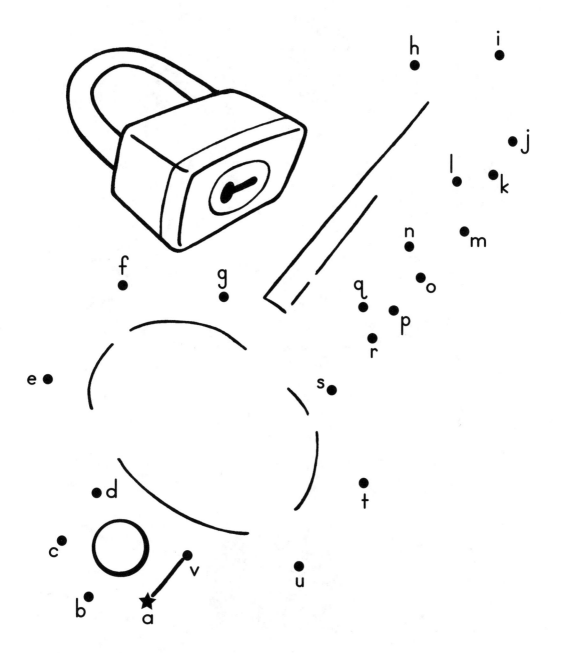

Busy Bees (a–x)

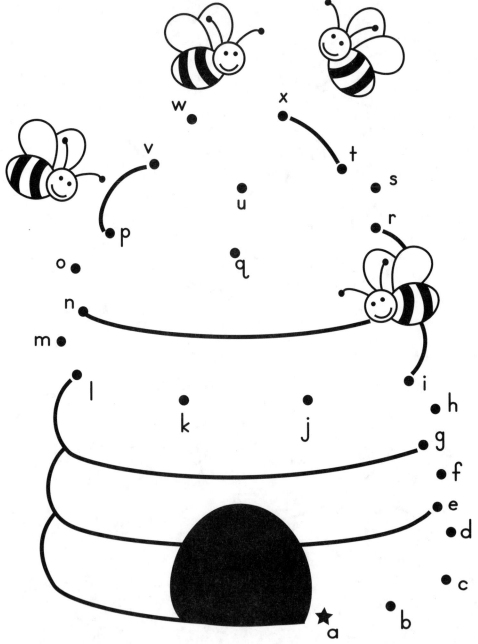

All Dressed Up (a–x)

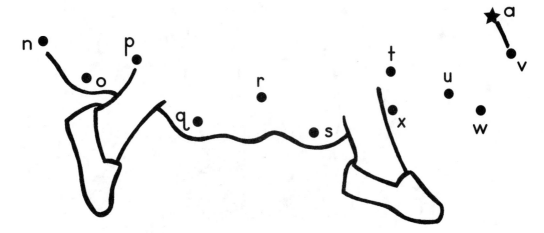

Wagging Tail (a–z)

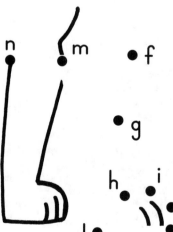

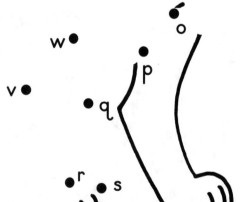

26

A Little Cub (a–z)

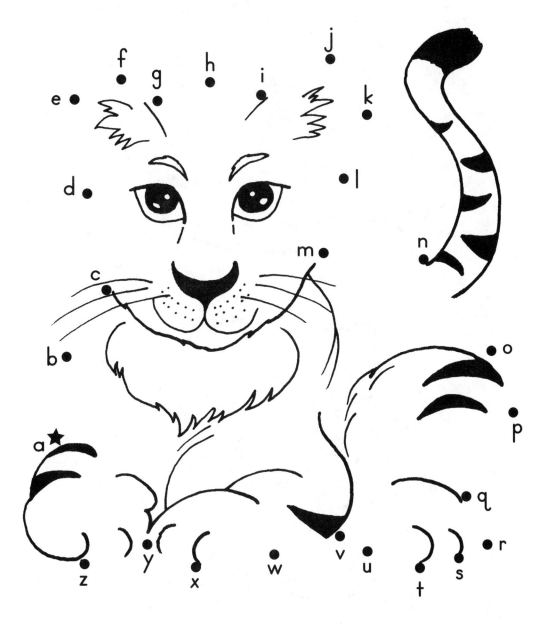

Where Is My Hat? (a–z)

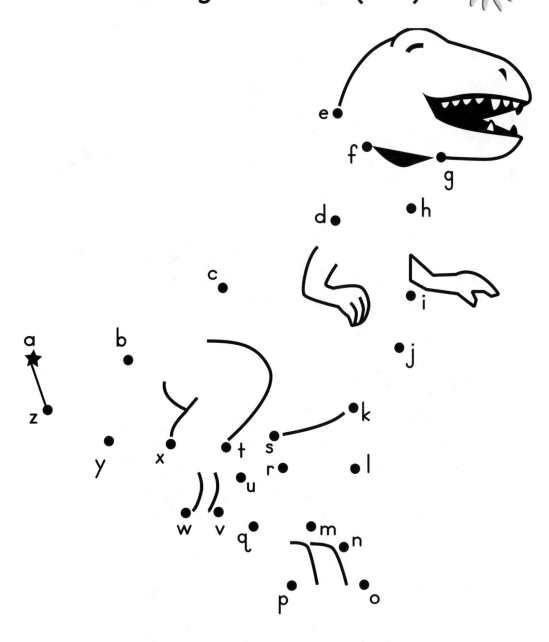

Dancing Dinosaur (a–z)

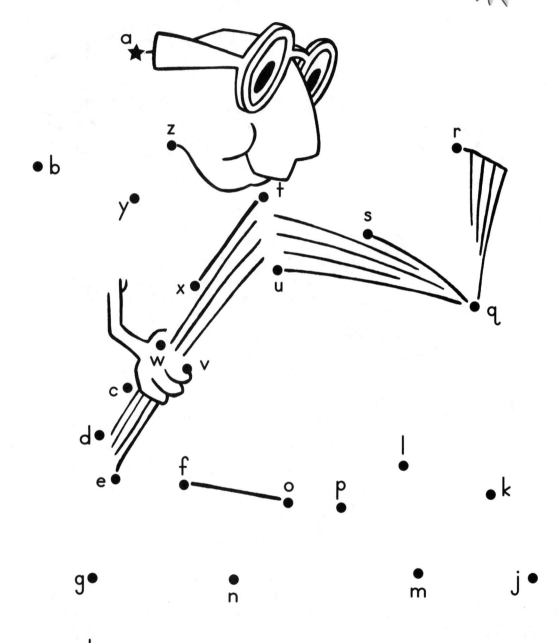

Reading Time (a–z)

Up in the Air (a–z)

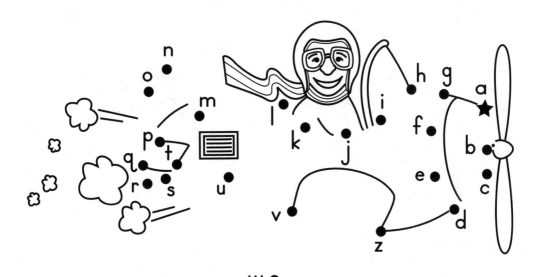

Letter Bear (a–z)

A Whale of a Tale (a–z)

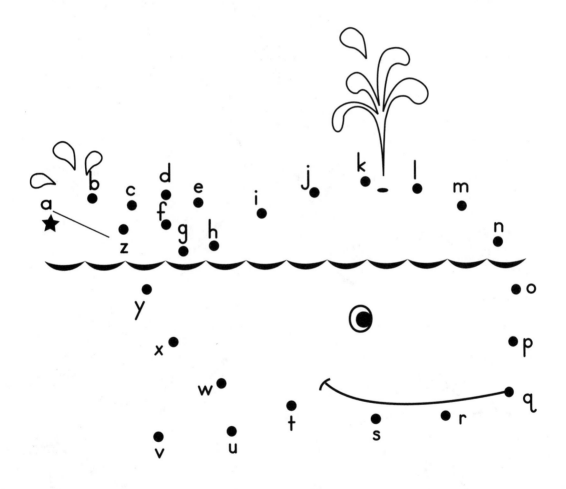

Moon and Stars (A–J)

School Bus (A–J)

SCHOOL

E

F

D

G

C

H

I

B

J

★
A

Clown Face (A–K)

Paintbrush (A–K)

Tiny Raindrops (A–O)

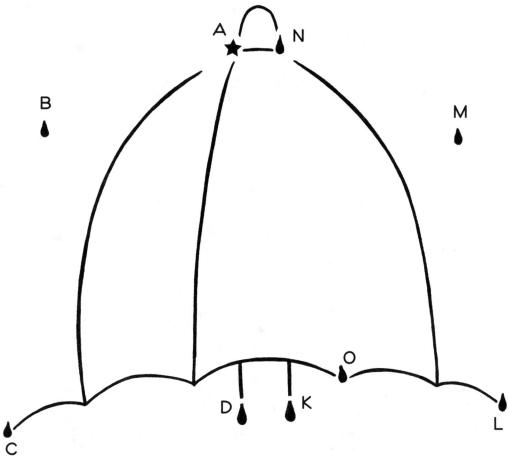

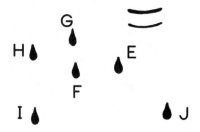

ABC Blocks (A–P)

Jack in the Box (A–P)

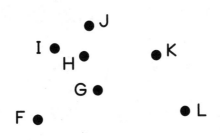

Ice Cream Cone (A–Q)

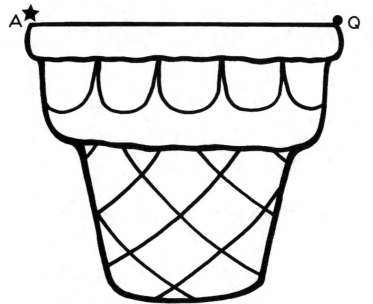

Fishbowl (A–R)

Swan (A–T)

Bowtie Bear (A–T)

T
S
A
B
C
D
R
E
Q
P
O
F
N
G
M
H
I
L
K
J

Raincoat (A–T)

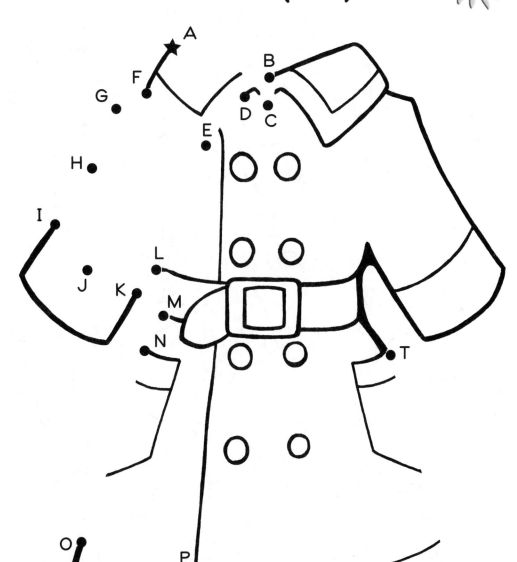

New Puppy (A–T)

46

Playing Penguin (A–U)

Guitar (A–V)

Ready·Set·Learn

Horse Trot (A–V)

Star! (A–W)

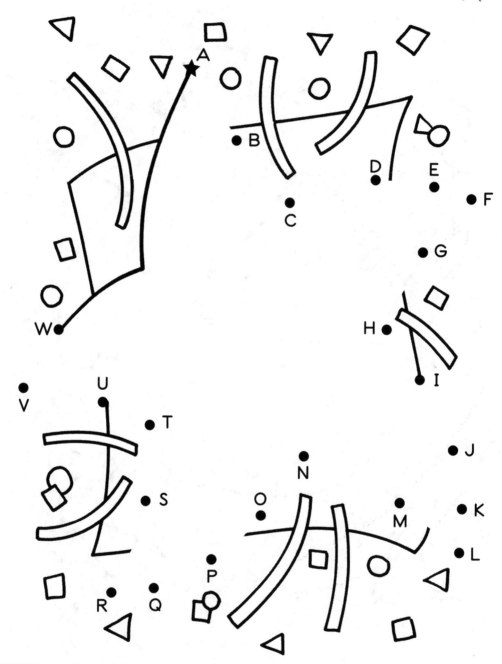

Football (A–X)

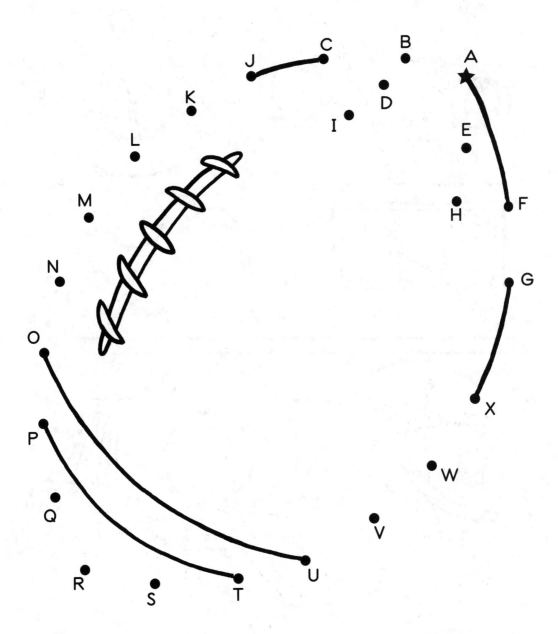

All Aboard (A–X)

52

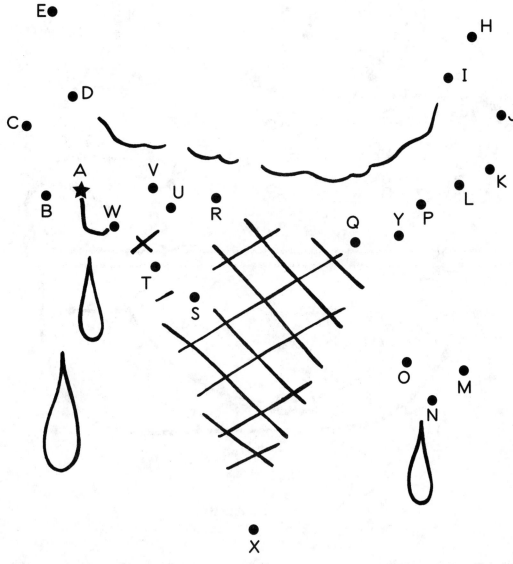

Ice Cream Cone (A–Y)

Ready·Set·Learn

F G

E

H

I

D J

C

A V U K
B W R L
Q Y P

X T
S

O M
N

X

Sitting Duck (A–Z)

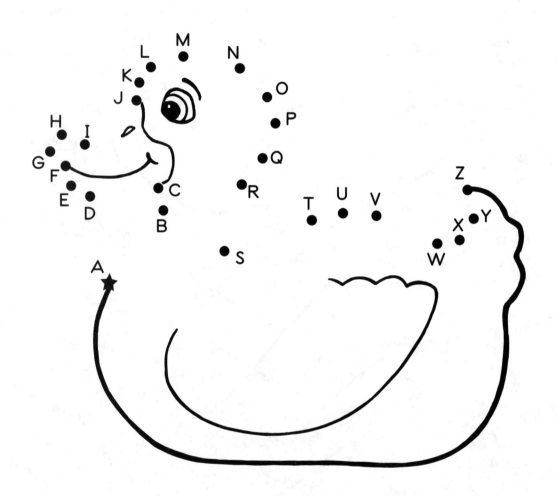

King of the Jungle (A–Z)

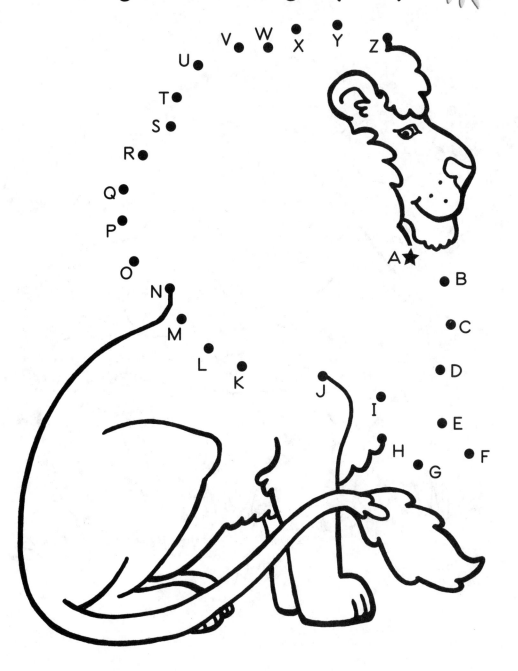

Cow (A–Z)

Under the Palm (A–Z)

Follow the Waves (A–Z)

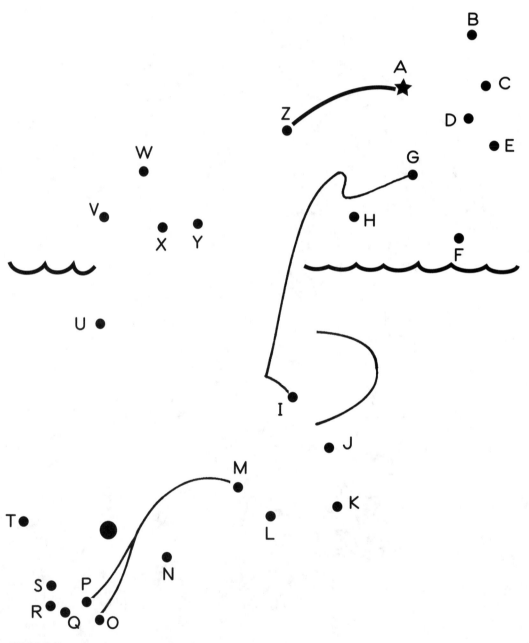

Robot (A–Z)

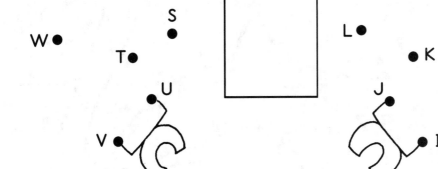

Cheese Is Good (A–Z)

Dancing Bear (A–Z)

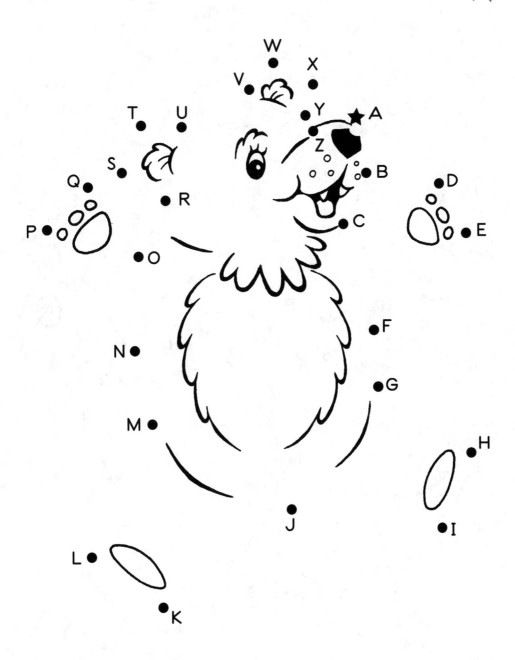

Ready·Set·Learn

So Slow (A–Z)

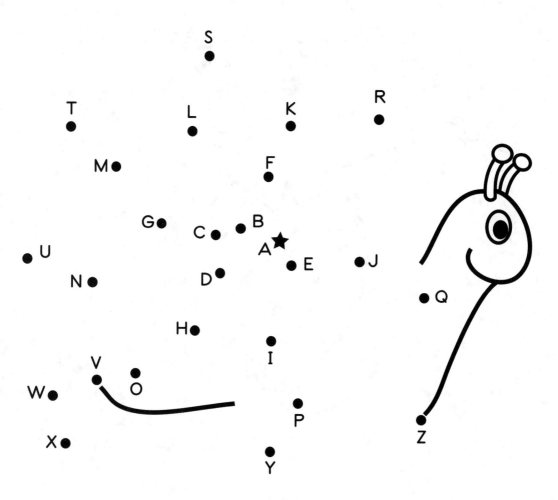

This Award
Is Presented To

_____

for

★ Doing Your Best

★ Trying Hard

★ Not Giving Up

★ Making a
Great Effort